ART OF THE JOURNEY

ORIGINAL POETRY & WORKS OF ART **BY DON TOCCO**

ISBN-13: 978-1-879094-99-4

Library of Congress Control Number: 2012947452

Copyright © 2012 by Don Tocco

All rights reserved. Published by Momentum Books, L.L.C.

117 West Third Street
Royal Oak, Michigan 48067

Printed in Canada

Book design by Stephanie Walters

Cover: Moon Mountain by Don Tocco

ART OF THE JOURNEY

ORIGINAL POETRY & WORKS OF ART **BY DON TOCCO**

SEVEN SHADOWS

This book is dedicated to my mother who encouraged me, my father who disciplined me, and my grandparents who loved me unconditionally. I am certain all talents are a gift from God, and true friendships make life worth living!

—Don Tocco

PREFACE

One summer morning my office phone rang. It was a young man calling to request a meeting to discuss his interest in teaching the Dale Carnegie Leadership Course. I was the Michigan franchise owner and looking to grow the business, so I agreed to meet with him.

My question to Don was, "Why do you want to be in our classrooms?" He stated his interest was in helping others, encouraging them to follow the human relations principles found in Dale Carnegie's book *How to Win Friends and Influence People,* and to stay positive in life. He had little to show by way of achievements in his own life, but his enthusiasm, sincerity, and passion won me over.

Indeed, he became involved for nine years and donated a great deal of time in our classrooms, assisting our instructors and helping more than a thousand adults improve their lives. I share this story because almost forty years later, he is still doing as much as possible to encourage others — from elementary age students to seniors — to try new things and improve their skill sets.

This brief background is evidence of a man determined and committed to helping others at many levels. It is no surprise he would develop his own artistic abilities and find a way to turn them into inspiration for anyone who seeks growth. Each of us can learn from the thoughtful content of his writing and observing the patience seen in his sculptures, unique paintings, and photographs.

You will find the book is organized in four distinctive chapters.

CHARACTER deals with the things that are noble and can be considered having virtue and integrity. The writer asks that we take time for enriching our mind and spirit. Using "The Measure of a Man" as an example, it challenges readers to be thoughtful in their approach to life by recognizing the sanctity of mind, body, spirit, family, career, friendship, and God-given talents. The poem "Black" encourages us to evaluate our empathy toward our fellow man.

SATIRE uses a poignant humor to remind us about the pitfalls and dangers of overreaching technology, industry going unchecked, and wars for profit, not true freedom.

NATURE is heralded through youthful eyes looking in amazement at a simple raindrop, the peace of a summer night, ocean breakers lapping a lonely shore, and a single leaf. Each of these poems can be reminiscent of a quiet moment that almost every person has enjoyed with nature.

INSPIRATION begins with the poem "Far Out," which recognizes every person is unique. The other works show us how to benefit from having a mentor. No one should live without vision and goals, and it is best to work toward success by understanding the process. We see that everyone should admire the talent of a gifted writer and how no one should die not having a "lighted soul."

This book is a reflection of the thoughts of a young man, and forty years later the same concerns are present. If we do not change our thoughts we are destined to repeat the past. Dare to follow your aspirations and you, too, will leave a greater legacy for the generations to come.

By looking back we understand. By looking forward we aspire for a better life.

—Ralph Nichols, November 2011

INTRODUCTION

Every book has a story, but every story doesn't have a book. **Good fortune** permits me to share the story behind this one. Growing up in the turbulent '60s was both a challenge and an opportunity. Dramatic changes were under way on many fronts, with an abundance of stress caused from historic moments like the **assassination** of President Kennedy and the potential of nuclear **annihilation** with Russia. We witnessed rapid advances in science with men soon to be walking on the moon; it was like science fiction coming to life. The **1967 Detroit Riots** took their toll, and the **Vietnam War** was under way. All this external drama — while trying not to lose touch with enduring truths, the beauty of nature, hope, and the **spirit of love** — helped shape who I am.

Art of the Journey is four media of artistic expression. Composing **prose and poetry** was my way of journaling, recording thoughts and feelings. This activity **began at age 17**, with most poems in this book written **before age 22**. The writings are a record of my observations of the social mood created by the war, disregard for ecology, a growing disrespect for the institution of marriage, the Freudian approach to psychology, and most of all, the need to stay focused on nature, optimism, and creative design.

Sculpting began innocently enough. One summer evening at age 21, I was at home and found a piece of clay on the kitchen counter. Three hours later a small bust was completed; done with a butter knife, teaspoon, and pencil. The bust drew a compliment from my family, and the power of praise was forever implanted in me. Five years later, I convinced my grandfather to sit for four hours while I did my first-ever sculpt of a real person. It was a wonderful way to honor him and became the inspiration to do the same for many terrific people in my life.

Many accomplished Americans have given me the privilege of letting me complete their bronze portrait. These special people are personal friends; among them are war heroes, internationally recognized corporate leaders, a Princeton professor who taught with **Albert Einstein**, a famous TV star who founded an international youth leadership program, a U.S. Navy captain, a Coast Guard officer, humanitarians, and entrepreneurs. Two of these sculptures are **currently on display** in the Automotive Hall of Fame in Dearborn, Michigan.

The **photographs** herein are selected from more than 20,000 made over the years. The choice to use photos from a one-day shoot on the majestic island of Maui, Hawaii, was done for the purpose of offering a single theme. The "Mother Nature" series is comprised of images that capture the waves of the **powerful Pacific Ocean**, layers of deep shadows, fading sunlight, sharp cliffs, and soft skylines.

The motivation to **paint** came late for me, in 2006. My mother was dying, a sad time for every child. One positive aspect of her last months was recognizing the wall space she had in her home needed some artwork. I volunteered that first painting and in her unique manner she said, "The colors don't quite match the room."

Over the final few months of her life I provided more than a dozen options until one was perfect. She loved the lady in the flowered hat, titled "Mysterious Woman."

The book is arranged with each poem next to a complementary art form. The visual component is intended to raise the richness of the overall message. Can you find the connection between each one? It is my **sincere hope** that your time spent perusing these pages is rewarded with enjoyment, learning, and inspiration to create your **own artistic expressions.** In truth, we are each engaged in our own unique journey throughout our lifetime, and **I wish you great success in the Art of _Your_ Journey.**

—_Don Tocco, November 2011_

CHARACTER

SATIRE

NATURE

INSPIRATION

RECOGNITION

WEST COAST WAVE (AM)

WHAT IS THE PRICE?

They were affluent
So, they were shopping
As they did more often than not
After all money is to be spent.

I stood near the window
The one they studied closely
They were considering a large purchase
I was sure by their tone.

Then came my first surprise
One said, "I wonder how much it is?"
I then wondered why price would be of any concern
Soon I was to learn.

They were rich — I told you that
Homes, boats, diamonds, and other good investments
Everything you could ever want
Even healthy looking.

Anyway, I was more than flattered
When they turned to me and chattered
"Excuse me, do you know the price of that
Precious item — the one up above?"

I looked at the top shelf, puzzled
Which one up above?
All I saw, was a poster —
That spelled — L-O-V-E !

—Don Tocco, 1968

PRICELESS

THE MEASURE OF A MAN

A man is not his mind
However, he shall use it to contemplate
It will be his vehicle for decisiveness
Sharpened, it will be as a surgeon's scalpel.

A man is not his body
But he must live within its limitations
Honoring it as his temple
It will serve him well.

A man is not his heart
Yet he will yearn to follow it
It will draw him as the flower draws the bee
He will live between its mountains and valleys.

A man is not his soul
While his soul will flourish in meditation and prayer
It will blossom with honesty, integrity, and love
It will sustain the voice of conscience.

A man is not his family
Yet, truly his wealth will be counted here
His home a castle, however exulted or humble
If he has earned love and respect.

A man is not his career
But his career will measure him by scale
It will stretch and dash him, too
Rewarding him for diligence and punishing for idleness.

A man is not his friendships
While without at least one true friend
He will live in a void
The silence will be deafening.

A man is not his talent
But his talents are a gift from God
If gone untapped — he shall endure
Only shallow and unfulfilled.

What then is a man?
But a sum total of each aspect
One and all as a symphony
Yearning to harmonize with the universe.

—Don Tocco, 1986

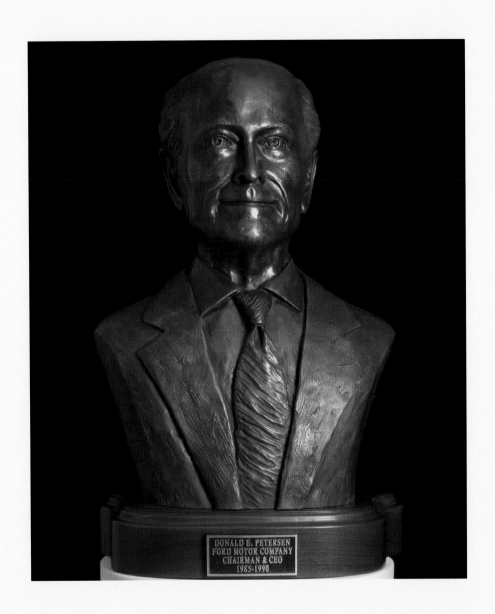

DONALD E. PETERSEN

Ford Motor Company

Chairman and CEO, 1985–1990

"BLACK"

As dark shadows cast themselves at length
Across an open space
I assure you, you'll not see
Much shadow on my face.

For as our sun glows innocently in the galaxy
Without malice it burns black on me
So now I ask a blind society
To take a look at something dear to me.

Stop ignoring and showing your back
Let's have a look at one who's Black
Let's look through a Black man's eyes
Can I see the color of the changing skies?

Live in a Black man's skin
Did I say, "I want black when I begin?"
I feel the biting wind if it's cold
As years pass by I, too, get old.

I blush 'cause I'm shy
And laugh and cry like an average guy
It's true I love a heavy sound
I clap my hands and stamp the ground.

What's wrong with the rhythm
We Black people have given?
I do not complain or despair
For I do breathe free the open air.

I, too, see the lighted star fall from
A stationed place
And I make my wish
As it tumbles through open space.

My wishes are the same as anyone
A good wife, a healthy son
Or time to rest
When my work is done.

So don't be mistaken by my color
That I'm not human like any other
About me there is nothing odd
For you see ... I, too, am a Child of God.

—Don Tocco, 1968

MYSTERIOUS WOMAN

ARÊTE* (A MESSAGE FROM ANTIQUITY)

Arête! Where have you been these past millennia?
Homer never intended your extended absencia
Reappearing again like a force forbidden
Your profound truth so long hidden!

Arête, you are the perfect word in Greek
Your ideas we shall ever seek
Apply your fire to heat and mold the metal of our youth
Expose them to your astounding truth!

Arête, strive for *character* first, it's true
Become *brave warriors* of *excellence* and *virtue*
Become the *best you can be*
Fearlessly, so the world can see!

Oh, Arête! Champion of this vital cause
In our efforts may we never take pause
A grand future begins right here
Listen as Socrates, Plato, and Aristotle cheer!

*Greek: Seek excellence in all things and become your best self

—Don Tocco, 2011

CAPT. JOHN LAVRAKAS
U.S. Navy (Ret.)
Served in World War II

LORD OF SMILES

Lord of smiles, I trust in thee for eternal laughter and joy.

I pray thee make me grateful and loving, full of smiles
for my brothers and sisters, weak and strong.

I know by smiling I can't go wrong.

Give me peace and comfort that I may sing your song
through loving eyes and a happy face.

Let me do my share to make this world a better place!

—Don Tocco, 1988

JOSEPH ANTONINI
KMART CHAIRMAN
1987 – 1995

JOSEPH ANTONINI
Chairman and CEO, Kmart Corp., 1987-1995

CHARACTER

SATIRE

NATURE

INSPIRATION

RECOGNITION

ON ECOLOGY

Have you noticed most recently
When looking up to see
On a calm, clear night
The stars aren't so bright?

So maybe you have thought
And, no doubt, you ought
That your eyes are getting bad
And how that makes you mad!

For just a few years back you'd spot
The stars formed a Roman Chariot
But this night you can't
And it's not because of clouds you can't.

Why, then, is the sky dull as hell
It has been answered and answered well
Yes, industry has answered it
The big dipper is ... full of it!

—Don Tocco, 1968

(Appeared in Wayne State University's *South End* newspaper, 1968)

POWER & BEAUTY

MAN'S MACHINE

Everyone's familiar with the robot
And you know they don't know a lot
But man built one
And made it like a son.

    He trained his machine to learn
    He programmed this robot to earn
    Why, he let it live in his house
    Allowed it to chat with his spouse.

The robot learned to think and feel
Some said it actually became real
Once it even cried and hid
It did everything as its master did.

    This machine slept and ate
    Tried once to get a date
    Played games just like a kid
    Yes, did everything its master did.

Then one day the machine flipped out
It had gone nuts — no doubt
So, men came and took him away
Yes, he did everything his master's way.

—Don Tocco, 1969

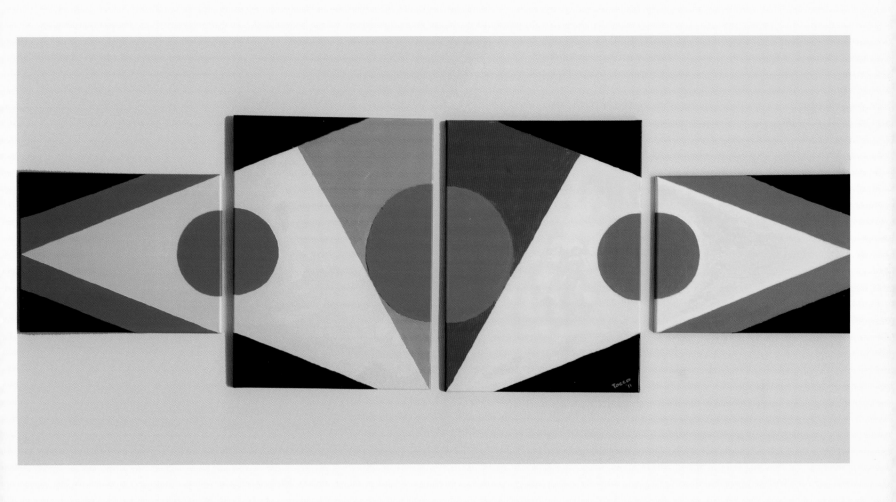

DOUBLE VISION

THE MARRIAGE CYCLE

How do you do?
Will you dine with me?
Will you dance with me?
Is there anything in this town you'd like to see?

I enjoy being with you.
I like you a lot.
I think I love you.
I'm sure.

Will you marry me?
You do love me and you will marry me?!
I'm sure this is the best day of my life,
I'm the happiest man in the whole wide world.

What's mine is yours and what's yours is mine.
We will share all these until death do us part.
Right?
Right!

Now what's wrong?
Oh, you don't like what I'm doing or the way I do it?
Where were you last night?
I see, out with the girls until 5 a.m.

Me ... Oh, out with the boys until 6 a.m.
Ya, playing cards.
Do you really hate me?!
A divorce, I suppose.

Until death do us part, HELL!
Now what do I share, but disgust for that which I loved.
How do you do?
Will you dine with me?

—Don Tocco, 1968

DIVORCED

THE WAR

I am still a child and being taught to kill
I cried when I left my home and girl against my will.

For the cause I turn a savage beast
As the demagogues cry, "It will soon cease."

As money flows in and blood flows out
It must be a fair trade without a doubt.

I got sick and cried as I'm not yet a man
When one good friend lost his head along with a hand.

This is a cruel and dirty war
It mars the soul and takes its score.

I hear them say, "World peace is the almighty cause."
But listen, the world claps a soft applause.

—Don Tocco, 1967

THE SHIELD

YOUTH

I am but a mere, simple cobweb —
hung up in a corner of the world.
My movements are determined by the physical
elements, as a slight breeze which might
shake me vigorously and threaten my security.
My form is normative for cobwebs.
Only varied by natural and artificial lighting,
making me large and ominous or obscure and
unentertaining. My existence seeming without
purpose. Yet I do not hinder or harm, help
or harass. YOU no doubt think me trite and
unnecessary, but honestly I am truly searching
for meaning. Surely there is more to existence
than being swept away by the long handled
mop of TIME.

—Don Tocco, 1966

WATER PLAY

A CIGARETTE TALKS

For me you'd walk a mile to buy
Because I calm and satisfy.

You carry me where'er you go
In summer sun and winter snow.

So, for your reward as a loyal friend
I'll watch you go — right to THE END!

—Don Tocco, 1968

Illustration by Ted Petok and "Save For Life" bank
based on Don Tocco's "A Cigarette Talks."
Tocco was recognized with a National Honor Citation
by the American Cancer Society.

CHARACTER

SATIRE

NATURE

INSPIRATION

RECOGNITION

SUMMER NIGHT

The moon shone full and it shone bright, vibrating and lighting the chords of my heart. There was more to be seen I knew, but time would not allow me to see — show me no more, because I love that which is before my eyes.

The clouds breathed pure gases as they moved lazily toward an unseen horizon. They were not massed and ominous, but rather very peaceful, silhouetting the moon like ocean breakers only without sound.

Nature's sounds vibrated as they talked amongst themselves. No doubt they discussed things of local importance, like the recently disease-stricken White Birch, or the presence of an uninvited figure — standing on and choking the life out of a tender blade of grass.

I could not see the wind this night. The leaves hung in a serene and almost melancholy manner waiting to be tickled by the tongue of a breeze, but no, they must wait. I stood thinking thoughts to be thought, embarrassed by the insects noting my peculiar manner. Surely my appearance seemed purposeless as I breathed deeply and wasted good oxygen.

This night was gentle, its warmth and comfort enveloped me and gestured reassurance. However, time passed and I was forced to leave this night. Closing my eyes I slipped into a night of my own. Was this a night I would remember, or was this a night that would remember me?!

—Don Tocco, 1968

HARVEST MOON

A RAINDROP

Born in a heaven of fleecy, billowy white
Sharing the boundless blue with winged creatures
And sailing warriors of man's Air Fleet, moving in
Gentle currents of up and down drafts.

Unnoticed I travel
My body is penetrated, warmed, and nourished by a
Radiant, robust ray of sunlight. I am charted
And most easily recognized in group form, but truly traveling alone.

Catching my breath in the clouds
Maturity has me boldly preparing my descent
I have in pear-shaped form, diagonally crossed
The distant expansion of space and met my task.

Molding mighty mountains, forging plush valleys
Refilling drying rivers with the wealth and
Abundance of myself and feeding the lakes and
Oceans of time with my presence.

Crystallized too, I have made my descent
Decorating naked nature in her winter state
Roundly and soundly have I plummeted, bouncing
Playfully and smarting slightly the surface of living things.

I have spawned the moisture of preservation
Falling and rising a billion times and more
Quenching the thirst of all …
And always leaving the rainbow of life.

—Don Tocco, 1967

CREATION

LONELY LEAF

Lonely leaf so way up high
Distant moon beyond in the dark blue sky
Evening is past, the sun is gone
Yet still, alone — you hold on.

What are you contemplating?
What must you see that intrigues you so?
Something deep and serious
Something giving you strength — so mysterious?

Look, all the other leaves have fallen
The only sound is the wind on the branches, so sullen.
No one there to share —
The crisp early winter air!

Hold- hold- hold
You are so bold — so determined
Has this long been planned?
Perhaps you are the message of one last stand.

Howling North winds,
Blinding white snow
Way up high I strain to see —
Yes! The last leaf is now free!

—Don Tocco, 2011

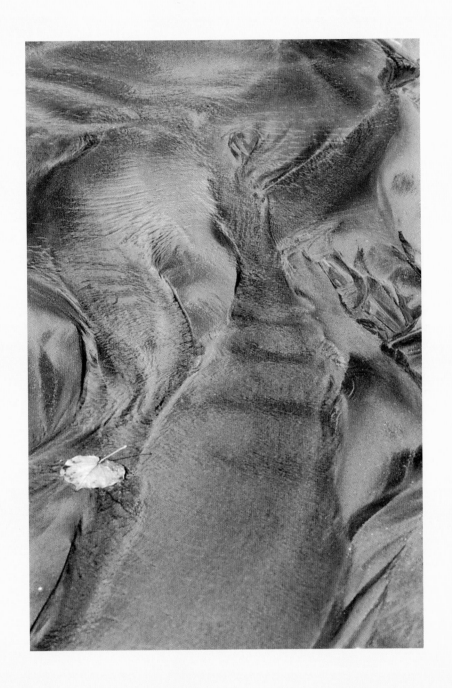

LONELY LEAF

A MAUI NIGHT

Was it a dream I had last night
That I walked the ocean shore?
With curling waves that broke
Over my feet with a familiar roar.

Note the moon — a perfect sphere
Did shine upon this scene
With clouds of art, so tall
So what could this all mean?

A humpback whale
With head and tail and ridges on its skin
Oh 10,000 feet in length and height
Floating in the sky oh what pure delight!

So high up in the sky, each star a dot
The ocean came rushing to my feet and washed them of the sand
So far we came to reach this spot
It is here, I wish to stand.

Stars shone so bright in the oval bowl
This special moment etched clearly on my soul
As we did commune in heart and soul
Ocean, moon, and man.

—Don Tocco, 1984

SEA MAIDEN

CHARACTER

SATIRE

NATURE

INSPIRATION

RECOGNITION

FAR OUT

Regardless of what some might say

The stars are **far out** and they're happy!

If they weren't they'd move in and be closer.

Regardless of what some might say

If **you are far out**

And happy

Baby, stay out!

Because being far out ...

Makes a lot of stars shine ! ! ! ! !

—Don Tocco, 1966

GALACTICA

THE SANDS OF TIME

The shifting sands of time,

That bury the poet and his rhyme;

The greatest structures lose their height,

As the sands creep on the winds of night.

Loud voices scream and shout,

But the brightest star will go out;

The hardest metals will rot and peel,

As into their pores the sand will steal.

You know the sands will crawl and shift,

They will bury the most treasured gift;

Blanketing all and taking their toll,

But alas! Never to touch the lighted soul.

—Don Tocco, 1968

TIME BANDIT

THE EAGLE/MENTOR

You who roam the free sky
And know the boundless open spaces
You who resent the confined arena
Where others are watched and judged in fear.

It is you, too, with keen vision and majestic flight
Daring to venture over foreign land and sea
Conviction and faith power your mighty wings
Then gliding on the currents of courage.

Only those with the eagle's heart
Can recognize the heart of another eagle
So you see my friend, we in fact fly together
In uncluttered space and quiet communion.

May we travel together ere long
Knowing the strongest wind cannot last
The darkest cloud will perish
Remembering we are a creature of the heavens.

Born to teach the hawk and tempt the lightning
Remembering the sun is our brother
The night our telescope to the stars
And the mountaintop our starting point.

—Don Tocco, 1979

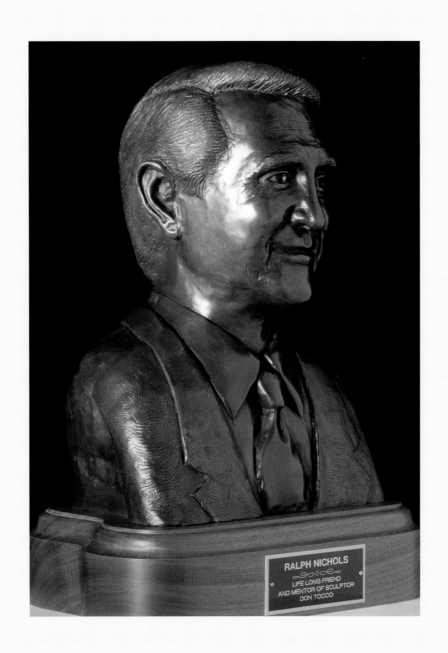

RALPH NICHOLS
U.S. Coast Guard Officer
No. 1 Dale Carnegie Franchise in the World: 1988

VISION — PASSION — OBJECTIVES

Without a vision the future is random.

    Without passion, life would be a broad gray sky.

Without objectives, we have no benchmark for measuring our successes.

    Were it not for hope and faith, we would never begin a task;

Lacking leadership, no one would dare follow.

    Short on courage — fear would win by paralyzing every idea

    In a bleak and frozen grave!

—Don Tocco, 1984

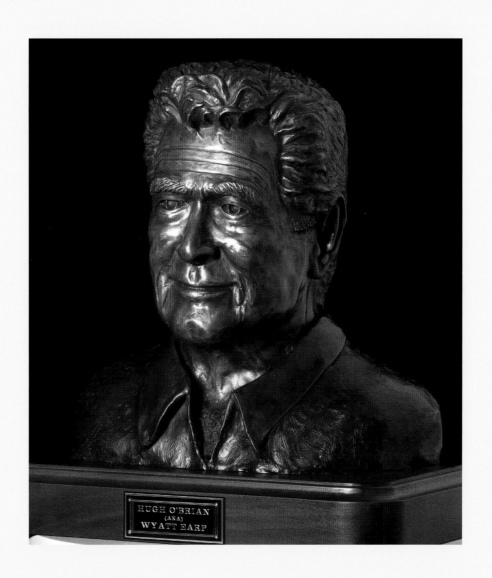

HUGH O'BRIAN
(A.K.A. TV's Wyatt Earp)
Founder, Hugh O'Brian Youth Leadership

HOW TO SUCCEED

How to succeed is not the question to ask,
It's rather how to think to conquer the task;
Think right — yes is easy to say,
But consequently to think right is the only way.

Know first which mountain you are to move,
Your direction mapped and your thoughts improve;
To see the end when it's not even near,
Is to focus your thinking ever so clear.

Laugh hardy when others harass you and scorn,
For failure they've thought since the day they were born;
Remember, too, that roads often swerve,
But remain strong in the helm and bend with the curve.

Your thoughts are your arrows and your heart is the string,
Remain sure with your faith and achievement will ring;
For the right way to think is how to succeed,
Think right and yours is inevitable success, indeed!

—Don Tocco, 1987

HAROLD "RED" POLING
Chairman, Ford Motor Company (Ret.)
Sculpture on display in the Automotive Hall of Fame, Dearborn, Michigan.

THE WRITER'S PEN

What guides the course of the writer's pen
Over the seas of verse?
How does he go where he's never been
And tell of blessing or curse?

From the temple of your roving soul
To the wizard's castle tower
You know he's never been there
But tells of it by the hour.

Could it be he's mystic
And boasts a sorcerer's power?
When all he need do is think
And write unceasingly by the hour.

He doesn't need a reason
To write of every season
He is intimate with raindrops
And knows their every worth.

The point of a pen in a writer's hand
It knows the thoughts of every man
He'll write ten long stanzas about a ray of the sun
Others might try, but write only one.

If you ask the writer though
What he thinks of life
You would be surprised to know
Simply he would say, "Beautiful is life."

—Don Tocco, 1968

JACK KRASULA

Founder, Decision Consultations Inc.

Humanitarian

CHARACTER

SATIRE

NATURE

INSPIRATION

RECOGNITION

THE ARTIST'S FIRST SCULPT, WHICH IS THE SIZE OF A BASEBALL, WAS DONE WITH A BUTTER KNIFE AND PENCIL AT THE AGE OF 21.

J. EDWARD LUNDY
Princeton Professor
U.S. Army Air Force
Original "Whiz Kid" and CFO, Ford Motor Company, 1947-1985
Sculpture on display in the Automotive Hall of Fame, Dearborn, Michigan

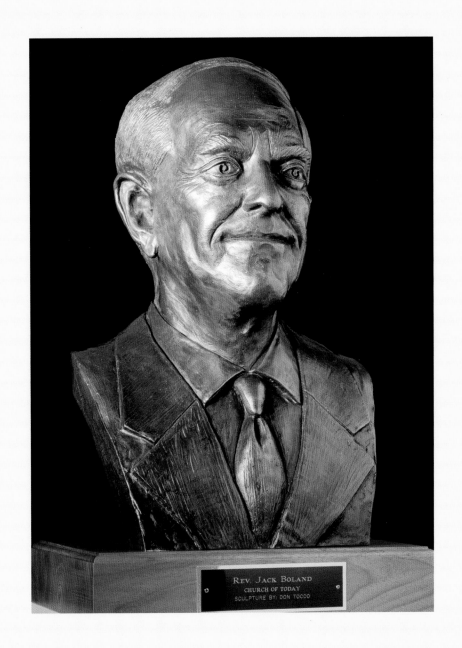

REVEREND JACK BOLAND

National TV Ministries

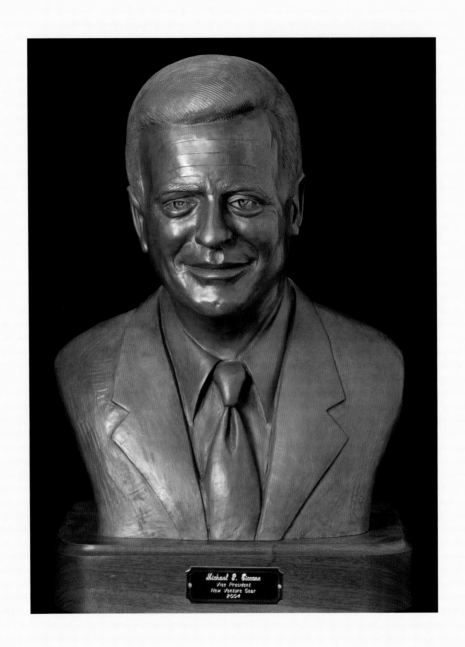

MIKE CICCONE
Director, Chrysler Corporation (Ret.)

L. BROOKS PATTERSON
Oakland County Executive of Michigan

ABOUT THE ARTIST

DONALD L. TOCCO is a businessman and the founder of D.L. Tocco & Associates Inc., a national marketing company. The corporation develops business for the heavy industrial construction industry. Starting business in 1974, the corporation has introduced its clients to more than 750 manufacturing facilities across the United States, Mexico, and Canada.

Don's passion for helping others grew in 1972 when he was invited to be an assistant instructor for the Dale Carnegie Leadership Course and Sales Courses, sponsored by the Ralph Nichols Corporation. He was involved in twenty-one separate classes over nine years.

Parlaying his communication skills, he donated considerable time to youth programs, including Hugh O'Brian Youth Leadership (HOBY) of Los Angeles, California, and was asked to be its keynote speaker for the World Leadership Congress in 1987. He was invited back twenty-three years in a row. His presentations have reached young leaders from every state in America and seventy countries.

In 1988, after personally seeing the benefits of inspiring young people in HOBY, Tocco founded the Youth Enrichment Series (YES), which was later recognized by the then General Motors EDS Corporation. YES is a program with powerful "real world"

tools for youth, presented by Don to fourth and fifth grade students in more than twenty-five elementary schools in Michigan. Students continue to write years later to recognize the value of the ideas presented.

He has spoken at America's major colleges and universities, including: Hillsdale College, University of Michigan, Michigan State, Johns Hopkins, Arizona State, The George Washington University, Rice, Spring Arbor College, Ohio State, and Tufts University. He has shared the podium with notable figures, including a past President and a past Vice President of the United States, a Nobel Peace Prize winner, senators, congressmen, industrial leaders, famous authors, and economists.

The combination of an enduring career serving the industrial marketplace has been balanced by a lifelong commitment to family, friends, community service, and faith in God. The artistry found on these pages is another facet of his love for beauty and zest for life. His main theme and goal in life remains helping others reach their ultimate potential.

NOTES

Acknowledgements

I wish to thank Ted and Mary Andras for their important input on the title and cover of the book. I am grateful for Nick Komic and Marzena Cintron, two excellent professional photographers, for providing photos of the sculptures and paintings for the book, Nick Komic having photographed all of the sculptures. Thanks to my secretary, Danielle St. Aubin, for her extra effort in making all of the printed materials perfect before submitting them to the publisher. My friend and longtime business associate, Steve Eick, was the ever-present sounding board for important changes in the organization of the book. Last, but not least, no better team can be found to organize, manage, and publish a book than my friends at Momentum Books in Royal Oak, Michigan.

Reproductions for Purchase

If any corporation or individual is interested in purchasing copies of either the paintings or photographs in this book, please contact the author at DonToccoArt@aol.com for pricing and delivery. Additional copies of this book may be purchased in the same manner.